Love Song
to
Mother

Adebola Abeni Omotayo

Love Song to Mother
© 2020 Adebola Abeni Omotayo

With pleasant colour pictures

Published by:
Sundaben Life Adjustment Consultants Press

Facebook Page:
Adebola Abeni Omotayo
http://fb.me/thewomanauthor

Dedication

To my Mother's mother who persuaded her daughter to have one more child against her initial decision to hang the boots after her fifth child. My grandmother's counsel was instrumental to my mother having the sixth child: Me!

To my Mother, Adunni Okin, obi uro, omo akin (Regal Adunni, indigene of Uro, child of the brave).

I saw you face the world with uncommon courage. You were a woman of depth who maintained a lovely heart till the end in spite of all that life threw.

I have never seen a wife of a polygamous man so loved and praised by the children of rival-wives: older rival-wives called you daughter, younger rival-wives called you mother, age mate rival-wives called you friend. Every in-law called you gracious.

In your own father's house you are the agent of unity. In the last neighbourhood where you lived, everyone called you grandma. In the last neighbourhood where you traded, your younger business partners and neighbours adopted you as mum.

In the last church where you worshipped, the earliest worshippers to arrive the church that glorious Sunday morning knew that something must have gone wrong with Grandma when they met the church dirty. They left the church for your residence, which was just a stone's throw away. One of them was a nurse, and her service that morning was to dress your body which had become too weak to house the soul; you gave up the ghost and could no longer go and clean the church with your live-in grandchildren, Bidemi and Yomi, in your characteristic manner.

Your sacrificial life remains a source from which I draw strength to stay on when the situation suggests otherwise.

I didn't know that an angel could come so humbly until one of the people you mentored described you as an angel in a eulogy at your funeral. How could I have lived with an angel without knowing!

Acknowledgement

This work is made possible by the Grace of God. I am therefore grateful to God for the inspiration and for raising helpers to assist in different ways in the course of producing the book.

I am grateful to my husband, Ambassador AGP Omotayo for his friendship and partnership in life and career tasks respectively.

I am grateful to Mr. Lawrence Oladele Ige of The Ekiti State Tree Growers Association for his assistance in compiling pictures for the book.

I say thank you to Johnson Adeoye Ogunleye and Chidebere Ife Kolawole for the professional desktop services offered in the process of producing the book.

I am grateful to all those who have contributed in one way or the other to the successful completion of this work.

Thank you all!

Preface

The mystery of motherhood astonishes an average woman too once a while, as it does men and girls, because a woman on motherhood duty is just a vessel for the divine will. As painful as the motherhood experience may be, every woman is drawn to it by something beyond her.

Despite submission to the divine will and the apparent associated pains, many women are only expecting joy in heaven. Poverty, misunderstanding, untimely death, ill-health are some of the innumerable factors that may prevent many mothers from knowing joy in a whole lifetime. Her heart aches, her heart bleeds yet even the closest persons to her upon whom her energy is being expended may never know exactly what her needs are. Unfortunately, her health fails or she dies without her heart ever knowing sustainable joy.

When the worst happens, everyone around her is the loser regardless of possible replacement options that may be available to fill the gaps created by her death.

Love Song to Mother is intended to help serenade every mother whose family comes across this book. A member of the family, daughter, son or mother shall come across this book and acquire it for the intended purpose.

Love Song to Mother sheds light on the innumerable roles of the mother particularly in the life of her child and since everyone is someone's child. Everyone shall therefore find this book affordable, to say thank you to their mother.

Where the mother is literate, it is a simple gift that serves as a letter of recognition and appreciation from the giver which the mother can read by herself and feel light from emotional burden and complex.

Where the mother is illiterate, the book serves the same purpose even though someone has to read to her a part of the book that she likes to listen to for lifting. The reader is free to replace Mother with their own mother's name to make the poem original in every hand that shall hold the book.

Where the mother has gone to join the league of mothers in heaven, a child shall find the book a suitable song to sing to the memory of their mother that she may smile as she looks down on her seeds on earth. A reader in this situation shall also insert the name of their mother wherever Mother is written to make the poem original to the mother being serenaded across the bridge.

A mother whose worth seems not to be recognized by anyone and on the verge of questioning the purpose of God for her life shall discover how endowed and recognized she is in the programme of God while singing to herself from this book.

A happy mother who happens to come across this book before her child finds out about it shall find the book useful for recognition and celebration of herself.

All mothers shall find Love Song to Mother invaluable as reading it is expected to energize her soul to love more and keep loving regardless of the situation. The lines reveal her real energy to upturn any threat that challenges her mothering ministry.

A father who loves his children and understands the office of his wife as the mother would also find this book a noble gift to the woman who made him father.

Everyone born of a mother would find the lines of this book useful to say "thank you mum".

Introduction

Love Song to Mother is a eulogy to celebrate motherhood. The long song is broken by twenty-six headings to present each characteristic of Mother distinctly. A reader may flow with the reading as a single elongated love song while the lines under each heading also qualify as a whole song.

The book is written in poetry form in order not to encumber the points with unnecessary literature. Some of the descriptions of Mother presented in this book derive from popular age-long sayings; for instance, the Yoruba call Mother gold. Some other descriptions derive from personal study and observation by the author. In addition to being privileged to watch her own mother bear the motherhood cross, the author had encountered many more mothers displaying the qualities described in this book. More importantly, being a mother has brought the experience down to her first hand beyond what observing and reporting could offer.

The book love Song to Mother specifically mentions the names of some outstanding mothers. Some of them have earned themselves a place in history; some of them are mentioned in connection to the outstanding children that they have given the world, while some are mentioned as a result of their display of incomparable love for which a mother is noted.

The lines in Love song to Mother consist of praises, teaching, admonition, encouragement, among others.

Attuned to Nature

Akoko tree

Newbouldia laevis

Newbouldia laevis (Akoko in Yoruba language) is Mother's friend and secret pharmacy from a long time: it is a broad spectrum medicinal plant from which Mother taps to aid fertility, stimulate labour, treat cough, heal chest pain, treat malaria, and treat infection, among other things. It is used to decorate a distinguished son or daughter during kingship coronation and chieftaincy. It signifies longevity; a topmost desire of Mother's heart.

1

The Inestimable Gold That Money Cannot Buy

The greatest connection exists in mother-child relationship.
No other can replicate the Mother role in her child's life.
Mother endures so much to ensure the foundation of a new life.
Mother nurtures the fusion through formation to zygote, embryo and foetus,
And then the child is born!
A bonding that transcends human comprehension.
The ship called Mother towers above ordinary,
A medium for the supernatural hierarchies' project,
Transporting earth-bound immigrants from realms beyond.
Mother's is an angelic mission.
Mothers are chosen from above and the anointing is priceless.
If you have a mother, you have got an angel nearby,
Your envoy to the heavens every now and then.
Your intercessor and the defender of your interests as you move about here below.

Mother is the shield of her child's glory.
She is the child's first food processor and feeder.
First covering and make-up divine,
First duvet and pyjamas combined,
First landlord and caretaker in one,
First bathroom and swimming pool integrated,
First nurse and care giver.
Mother too is first school and first learning-mate.
How much will buy a mother?
Never, child had no money before having Mother;
You have a mother first who sets you on the path to having money.
Mother is indeed the inestimable gold money cannot buy!
Mother is the most precious jewel anyone can have.
Some metals may be precious,
None is as durable and worthy as Mother.
Not bronze, not silver and not the element called gold.
Neither diamond nor platinum comes near the worth of a mother.
For the value of them is monetary,
And there they are on shelves for sale.
In case of loss, they are replaced.
Again and again money does it.
Ooh you haven't seen duplication and imitation?
Nothing in this world compares to Mother,
She can neither be duplicated nor imitated.

She is the gold upon which no monetary value can be placed.
Mother cannot be bought off shelf in a store.
A mother lost to death is not dead;
Not even asleep,
Her love, teachings and spirit live for aye,
A legacy they remain for generations down her line.
Mother is the real precious jewel that can neither be bought nor acquired
nor abandoned nor divorced;
No court of law has the jurisdiction to divorce a mother from her child.
And no tricks can be played with the DNA.
The one who carried you in pregnancy is mother forever.
Gold of inestimable value that money cannot buy she is!

Coconut tree

Cocos nucifera

Cocos nucifera is the scientific name for the Coconut tree. The fruit of this tree commonly called Coconut is edible in its raw state yet Mother processes it in many different ways for even more delicacies. There are other parts of the coconut tree that are edible as food and as medicine. Parts of the coconut tree are also made into utility objects employed in Mother's chores.

The coconut fruit is perceived as a wonder and it is therefore used as a prayer object evoking the power that made it possible for water to be enclosed within the coconut in a wondrous way. Mothers in some climes appease the spirit of the child by bringing together neighbourhood children in a birthday-like celebration where native small chops are shared; raw coconut cuts are usually part of the food composition. Each child who collects a portion of the food composition prays for the child being celebrated to Mother's delight.

2

Divine

The creator replicates heaven and earth within
mother.
Her womb is the heaven where we were.
Her heart is the ever open, ever current temple,
Where she intercedes for the child.
Prayers and sacrifices she continually offers;
To ensure the success of her mission as a channel,
A channel for the will of God,
To bring another soul down and nurture to maturity.
She is the bearer of the narrow path,
Which many seek in worship houses.
Hers is the narrow path,
That leads to heaven and brings to life.
Her mammary glands;
The fountain of the living water that sustains life.
The law of procreation becomes real through mother.
Mother is the oracle who tells the man first,
That he is going to become a father.
To come to pass or not,
Is dependent on the Woman's wish, choice and
decision.
Her child's growth, development and achievements,

Are first created by imagination on the shrine of her heart.
Mother's womb is the haven and heaven,
That midwives can attest to.
There is no deity like Mother.
Mother must accept the task of a carrier,
Before the heavens could be praised for another release.
Which deity shall a child therefore know without the Mother?
Mother is the ally that helped the work of the unseen offices,
To bring down here a willing soul.
Her womb, hormones, glands and organs are more mysterious,
Than deities that exist,
In lifeless frames of wood, bronze and iron.
The mystery of motherhood is beyond man like legends and myths,
Yet with us here as reality that we can see.
Mother is a child's head in pregnancy and a head and monitoring angel she remains,
All life through.
Mother narrates child's own utterances, movements and activities,
To the then child-actor,
Who now is an adult with faded memory.
Who else could know you,

More than you know yourself,
If not an oracle?
The child Mother blesses is blessed and others are
less.

Neem tree

Azadirachta indica

The Neem tree is known as Dogoyaro in Nigeria. The roles of trees are generally similar to Mother's roles; trees bear fruits, they provide shade and protection. Neems, member of the mahogany family are drought-resistant just like Mother is resilient.

3
Loving

There are two ways to describe a mother's love;
The lower and the closer cases.
The lower case is to liken a mother's love,
To how a person likes self.
The closer case is nearer the truth;
It is to liken Mother's love,
To how God loves us.
No one else can serve as much sauce on one's meal as
one's own mother.
She is eager to see her child grow.
Her child's growth is her joy and her strength.
Her child's growth is her growth too.
And her child's growth is her pride.
She is happy to see her child grow strong,
For her child's strength is her strength.
She gives everything it requires,
To see her child grow strong.
She is ready to give more than the child can take,
That her dream on the child which the child sees not,
May come to pass as fast.
Her child's growing capacity to take more and more,
Is Mother's delight.
To sacrifice her portion for her child's plate,
Is her pleasure any day.

The extra portion on the child's plate,
Is a catalyst to produce the picture,
The picture of her child she is waiting to see.
She won't eat when her child is yet to eat.
Her child's lack of appetite is mother's displeasure.
Will a step-mother, a friend's mother, a foster mother
or even a grandmother do or be all these?
Only Mother will!

Osun tree

Pterocarpus osun

Pterocarpus osun is simply called Osun in Yoruba and Camwood in English. Osun has served Mother for centuries by its cosmetic and medicinal parts to treat different conditions affecting both young and old. The tree has an undeniable connection with childcare in parts of the world. It is a traditional pedicure ingredient for brides among the Yoruba. Mother applies Osun on babies to treat skin irritation, thereby making her children's skin smooth and attractive.

4
Unforgettable

Pipe smokers do not forget matches.
The river does not forget its source.
One who suddenly forgets who the mother is has been cut off from self,
Who shall heal such?
Shall anyone forget the host who bore one within at a time of total incapacity?
Shall anyone forget the vessel by which one is brought forth to visibility?
Shall anyone forget the one who nurtured one to emotional and mental consciousness?
Shall anyone forget the one who taught one how to express oneself?
How on earth can the equation of a person's existence be balanced without the initial factor?
All hail Mother, the prime factor!

Banana Plant *(image-asset)*   *(banana+flower)*

Musa acuminata

The parent banana plant dies to be replaced by its sucker, like mother leaves child behind as descendant.

5
Source

Has anyone said that Terah the son of Nahor,
the son of Serug conceived Abraham?
Ask the sages and you will learn about Amatlai the
daughter of Karnebo!
Who would have known Jesus without Mary?
Who would have known Muhammad without Aminah
Bint Wahb?
Who would have known Augustine Patricius without
Monica of Hippo?
Who would have known Obafemi Awolowo without
Efunyela?
Who would have known Olusegun Obasanjo without
Ashabi?
Who would have known Charles the Prince of Wales
without Elizabeth?
Who would have known Barack Obama without Ann
Dunham?
Who would have known John D. Rockefella without
Eliza?
Who would have known Ben Carson without Sonya?
Who would have known Bill Gates without Mary
Maxwell?
Who would have known anyone without Mother?

Mother's belly protrudes to herald the coming of another soul in human form.

The belly of a pregnant woman is the heaven so near to see, touch or feel, and it is so real.

Heaven exists within Mother and child-bearing drives home the point.

O precious blessed mother, The Source!

Apple_tree_with_fruit-1

Malus domestica

The apple tree as a symbol of fertility reveals external beauty as indicated from within.   The apple tree represents internal and external beauty just as Mother's works of love reveals the beauty within.

6
Beauty

Mother is beautiful in her heart.
Mother is beautiful in her ways.
Mother is beautiful in her speech.
Mother is beautiful in her care.
Mother is beautiful in her prayers.
Mother is beautiful by her endurance.
Mother is beautiful by her patience.
Mother is beautiful by her understanding.
Mother is beautiful by her consideration.
Mother is beautiful by her sacrifice.
Mother is beautiful by her selflessness.
Mother is beautiful by her faith.
Mother is beautiful by her hope.
Mother is beautiful by her trust.
Mother is beautiful by the support she renders.
Mother is beautiful by her skills.
Mother is beautiful by her industry.
Mother is beautiful by her courage.
Mother is beautiful by her strength.
Mother is beautiful by her strength of character.
Mother is beautiful by her forgiving spirit.
Mother is beautiful by her tenderness.
Mother is beautiful by her accommodation.
Mother is beautiful by her intelligence.

Mother is beautiful by her insights.
Mother is beautiful by her foresight.
Mother is beautiful by her intercession.
Mother is beautiful by her steadfastness.
Mother is beautiful being mother.
A mother is the beauty that decorates her child's life.
Without a mother's inputs,
A child's life turns out less beautiful and less meaningful than it could have been,
And it may be shattered because no one truly cares.
Mother, O beautiful Mother!

Igi Arere

Triplochiton scleroxylon

Triplochiton scleroxylon is commonly called Obeche or Arere in Yoruba. The wood is widely used for interiors to make Mother's home comfortable and classy. Its parts are edible and medicinal.

The tree is an accommodating creature which allows silkworms to dwell and feed on it. The larvae of the silkworms are a good source of protein. The cocoon of the larva is the silk with which cloth is woven. Even the decaying wood accommodates the growth of mushrooms.

Triplochiton scleroxylon is preserved in plantations to serve as shade trees for cash crops like cocoa. It shares Mother's attributes of accommodation, provision and protection.

7

Empathiser

Mother is the unique counsellor,
That charges no fee.
The officer-on-call,
Without time limits and off days.
The proactive consultant that envisages the issues,
While the concerned plays away.
The permanent adviser,
That never gets frustrated and seeks not public notice.
The prayer warrior that remains standing even when the battle appears as to the death.
The supporter that feels the pains than the child affected.
No matter what the situation turns out to be,
Mother is ever standing, ever accessible and ever available.
Hail Mary the wife of Joseph the carpenter,
She was there at the cross with her son Jesus!
Hail Saint Monica, the mother of Saint Augustine;
Her sinner son ended up as a saint but the whole of her strength was the price paid!
Hail Adunni Atoori-bi-Opo, despite fierce psychic battles of polygamy,

She taught her children love and truth,
She conquered all by love,
And her step-children too call her blessed.
A most gracious description of "An angel" she earned,
As oration at her burial for she was all-love!
Hail Asabi Adedire,
Her kidney meant nothing if her son would live,
Not knowing that Abraham Adewole,
The Ife boy in Michigan would give up the ghost still,
And she gave it up!
Who can know this mother's pain?
What each mother feels, each mother knows!
Sweet is your memory Asabi,
Your kidney wasn't given for nothing,
It was given for love!
Hail Mama Rabi Olobi,
Rabiatu Funmilayo of the golden city,
Where the Olohan reigns supreme.
She faced everything that life brought with courage and calmness.
That her friend married her husband meant peace still,
Teaching her children love and courage until the fourth generation.
And the whole town called her Mother!
All hail Mother!

Palm tree

Elaeis guineensis (Palm tree)

As the human palm divides into fingers, *Elaeis guineensis* has its fonds divided into leaflets and it's called palm tree. It is a cash crop that dies not because of its resistance to harsh conditions and its dispersal methods, no wonder many refer to it as eternity tree.

Every part of *Elaeis guineensis* is suitable for commerce as a result of its usefulness. Palm oil extracted from the flesh of the palm-fruit is a necessity in many African cuisine recipes. Palm oil also symbolises ease just like the female gender, the gender of Mother symbolises ease. In addition to palm oil, very old palm trees secrete sweet palm wine just like mother's breast secretes sweet milk. The palm kernel inside the palm fruit is an age-long cosmetics ingredient from which medicinal salve is extracted to soothe the skin of Mother and her child.

8
Sweet Mother's Glands

Mother's gracious mammary glands,
Sweet and sustaining.
No other glands satisfies hunger like these,
Refreshing and thirst-quenching.
Mother feeds and nurture by breasts and by labour.
The love in her heart triggers her glands,
Her glands secrete love,
Her glands secrete power.
Her glands secrete authority,
Her glands secrete compassion.
And just like breast-feeding,
All of her glands nurture.
Mother toils day and night as the taps of her glands
are prompted.
Having those glands secreted brings relief to her
child,
From hunger or worry.
The secretion of her glands to nurture her child
works out relief,
And the relief by her secretion is invaluable.
Nurturing continues for as long as she lives
regardless of her child's age.
In fact, regardless of the mother's age too.

Before you understood hygiene, Mother was in charge.
She saw to what you ate, drank, and wore.
She found, she washed and she rinsed.
She guided, she guarded and protected.
She thought for you before you could think for yourself.
When you start to think, she thinks ahead and as a real adult, she thinks with you.
She dreamed of you, dreams for you and she will dream on and about you.
Your wisdom and courage derive from her nurturing, tutoring and mastership.
The farther apart from your mother, the more the task you will have to perform alone,
And the more you sweat alone.
O sweet mamas' glands!

Kola nut tree

Cola acuminata

Cola acuminata is priced for its fruit, the Kola nut, which is recognised in many regions as a symbol of hospitality and friendship. The fruit of this evergreen tree is also believed to ward off disease and even death. It is presented for sharing at significant occasions as a show of love and trust.

It is one of the most significant items with which blessings are offered at a marriage ceremony for the bride and groom. Similarly a new baby is offered prayers with Kola nut during the naming ceremony. Though all trees bring forth money, Kola nut is special. Many mothers have brought giants out of their children by giving them the best education possible with proceeds from their Kola nut business. The maiden that would be Mother is blessed with Kola; Mother's seed is blessed with Kola too.

9

The Cursed

Ignore that voice, child,
For it is the voice of the accursed.
It seeks to anger Mother to errors,
And targets the child as instrument.
Above the tricks Mother is,
Yet the voice tries harder,
Seeking lives to destroy.
Who art thou,
Whispering "disobedience"
When Mother teaches "obedience"?
Why wouldst thou highlight "lack",
When Mother preaches "endurance and hope"?
Mother teaches "perseverance",
And the voice screams "delay"!
She teaches "responsibility",
The invader whispers "freedom".
When she says "hard-work",
The secret voice entices with relaxation.
Against her lessons in diligence,
The child hears "ease".
When she says "vision",
The invader parades television.
When she says "decency",
The thief of minds says "It's a choice".

She says "education",
The thief broadcast short-cut options.
When she says "peace",
The intruder gives reasons to worry.
Many battles Mother had won,
Before the child came of age.
She sat and watched the infant head,
And wept for fear of death.
At every stage she had conquered,
But the enemy waits to use the child.
Who shall win this round of battle?
Mother is here as guard and the pole of light shall win!
The provocation notwithstanding,
Mother guards her own heart.
She does her crying in the rain,
And bridles her tongue,
Binding the tempter from within.
Who art thou, O force,
Pitching child against Mother?
Two poles are contending,
Over a child on mission.
The pole of Light is a reality,
But thou darkness an illusion,
That shall vanish forever!
Mother is of the Light pole.
Mother is pro-creation and pro-life,
And for life and light she stands,

Loving, caring and cherishing.
She sat and watched the child's infant head.
The devil seeks whom to destroy,
And targets the love between mother and child to spoil.
Mother and child?
What daring devil?
Ugh! Shame on the devil!
Real mothers are above thy tricks.
She will not get her moral strength punctured.
Though she mimics anger,
She shall not curse,
The pranks notwithstanding.
And though the devil may try the naïve child,
But mother is at the gate and her defense prowess is divine.
She shall not give in,
She shall not miss it.
When the devil thinks a channel he has got in the child,
Mother changes strategy,
She loves, she cares, she counsels,
In understanding and patience.
In silence and meditation, her spirit searches on.
For her, the devil's seeds must die!
This heart must be saved,
The heart of her precious child.
And the child's spirit must be free.

The child's heart must be delivered,
That mother and child may reap gains,
From leadership,
And from obedience,
And above all from pure love.
The negative pole recognises Mother,
A pro-creation vessel,
The creation which the devil targets for destruction.
The devil knows that a child must not be cursed by Mother.
Yet Mother is for love.
Flee from the accursed devil.
The devil is the cursed,
Who seeks more to be cursed.
Flee, flee, child of purpose!

Odan tree

Ficus thonningii

Ficus thonningii, called "Odan" by the Yoruba, serves humanity by its leaf, fruit, fibre, bark, fluid, wood and roots. The standing tree provides a shade for group meetings and a shade for relaxation and recreation for anyone who comes under.

Its all-round usefulness presents in nature a semblance of Mother's resourcefulness.

10

Who Are the Blessed?

Blessed is a mother at her duty post.
Blessed is a mother diligent in her role.
Blessed is a mother tilling in tears for she shall reap in joy.
Blessed is a patient mother.
Blessed is a forgiving mother.
Blessed is a mother who holds on to her fruits,
Regardless of the weight of her burdens.
Blessed is a mother who will not seek safety in flight leaving behind her fruit.
Blessed is a mother who shepherds her fruits like the mother hen shepherds her brood.
Blessed is a mother who hides her child from the abrasive elements of this world;
Oh yeah, like the mother hen hides her chicks from hawks.
Yes, like the mother hen hides her chicks in the dark cave of feathers underneath itself.
Blessed is a mother who feeds her fruits before satisfying her own hunger.
One who has got a mother is the blessed.
One who appreciates Mother is doubly blessed.
One who takes care of the mother becomes blessing.

Those who honour their mother celebrate themselves.

One who heeds the mother receives unending blessings.

These are the blessed.

One who has got a mother appreciates not the worth;

Ask someone who has got no mother.

Agaricus_bisporus-800x445

Agaricus bisporus (Mushroom)

Hard-working Mother-Earth is a giving planet that is capable of bringing substance out of nuisance. Imagine beautiful mushrooms emerging from decaying logs! So much simply springs forth for the use of human race, and the supply is endless like the flow of love for her child is eternal in Mother's heart.

11
She Suffered Hardship

Oh yeah, she did!
Mother suffered hardship.
Shall we talk of mothers betrothed against their own will?
Shall we talk of the vulnerability of young girls in search of purpose or mere daily bread?
Shall we talk of the torture by husbands who came originally for some ignoble missions?
They got caught up in the web of responsibility against their will,
And in turn intimidate the lady whose presence challenges their waywardness.
Shall we talk of the oppression by in-laws?
Shall we talk of duly married brides who could not conceive early?
Shall we talk of their encounters in their search to peel off the "barren" tag?
Shall we talk of the painful treatment to which many are subjected to achieve conception?
Shall we talk of the horrible things many ingested to get pregnant?
Yes, the reality behind many pregnancies is better left imagined.
And if you disregard all of these

Let's talk about the real things...
Let's talk about pregnancy
How much can anyone imagine?
From the fusion of the gametes which propels bewildering hormonal changes,
As the sibylline movement commences to defend the territory,
That the formation may remain on course,
To a point in time that no one knows,
In mothering, no comma, no pause.
Yes, prophesies will melt in the light of day,
But love with us will forever stay.
Every soul released to the earth is an embodiment of divine love,
And this Sibyl in flesh feels the pains of the process,
Yet the mission as a courier of love is as prophetic as no other,
It's a mission that must be accomplished.
While some sleep like the civet,
Many others are just restless day and night.
Some become voracious and gluttonous,
Others suffer loss of appetite.
The body keeps calling for food in some cases,
Others keep throwing up everything ingested as the body fights on.
While some have their lips flaking,
Others can't stop saliva from drooling.

Sitting, standing, lying down and walking all become difficult for some.
Those who experience sudden energy surge in the second trimester,
Won't have the unlimited freedom to go all out;
Old wife tales, doctors' warnings, midwives' counsel are all there policing.
She can't be lazy; she can't prove strong,
And it continues for nine months.
What about the D-day?
How much can anyone write, how much can anyone say?
No doctor has got the word to describe labour pain.
Oh dear, childbirth is no cakewalk!
And how can anyone describe post-partum pain?
Ooooh no, the boat has been rocked!
The table has been shaken!
The setting has been tampered with!
While some things have gone beyond elastic limits and would never return to status quo,
Some regions are suffering exhaustion, replenishment must commence ASAP!
Some walls and surfaces have been bruised, other things have been torn.
Against possible invasion, security must be mounted!
Horribly smelling antibiotics to the rescue,
So much Mother must swallow,
All these constitute pain.

And the way to healing is still characterised with pain!
Yet nurturing the baby can't wait.
Fun times come to standstill and career is on suspension.
Yet bills will rise!
When shall this labour end?
When the mother dies of course,
For she is needed for her grandchildren too.
Yet other missions must be fulfilled.
What each mother suffers each Mother can tell.
No child can repay the angel called Mother,
For her labour from inception to delivery alone,
For that alone is huge!
All hail Mother, the model of endurance,
The icon of perseverance,
Most loving, most patient.

dove-2516641_1280

Dove

The dove represents maternal quality of love. It also symbolises peace and tranquility.

12
The Counsellor

When every other one blames,
Condemns, rejects and judges you,
Mother stays and listens.
In understanding, she digests and empathises.
She continues to identify with you,
No matter where the pendulum swings.
The child's filament, taster and guinea pig Mother is!
She foresees, she foretells and weighs all the sides.
She then warns by her insights all in her child's interest.
She would have the time and be available,
In sickness, judgment and sentence.
She prays that you would be affluent lest you go lacking.
She consults, begs, pleads and appeals,
She sacrifices and appeases, all on your behalf.
Prices in cash or in kind she would pay,
On behalf of her child.
She would rather die than her child dies.
She counsels herself to leave while you live,
For to her, you are her glory behind.
Whatever happens to a child affects the mother and many times,
Deeper than the child.

A mother does not just sympathise;
She takes over the burden and the pain,
Of her beloved child's issues.
Mother, a lovely counsellor.

Faces of Love

Founder

Maryam Babangida (1 November 1948 – 27 December 2009)

Nigerians love Maryam Babangida for her love for them which she so vividly expressed by her commitment to the development of the womenfolk; everybody's mother. As Nigeria's First Lady between 1985 and 1993, Maryam Babangida launched many programmes to improve the life of Nigerian women.

She founded the Better Life Programme for Rural Women under which many cooperative societies, cottage industries, farms, shops, markets, women centres and social welfare programmes came into being. The Mariam Babangida National Centre for Women's Development in Abuja, Nigeria was established for research, training, and mobilization of women towards self-emancipation.

She networked with the first ladies of many African countries, shedding light on possible areas of impact that could make their first-lady role more effective. She remained instrumental to the socio-economic development of women in Africa far beyond her husband's presidential regime. Many community and commercial programmes that are still running across Nigeria today would trace their foundations to Mrs. Babangida's initiative.

Many women who would never have gone beyond their tiny communities enjoyed overseas travels by The Better Life Programme for Rural Women which sought to promote their skills and wares at trade fairs across the globe. The lots of those privileged women improved to the benefit of their children who enjoyed better feeding, better health care and better education. Maryam, a Mother and a destiny helper to many mothers.

13

Pilot

As automobile drivers differ from the vehicle,
Pilots differ from the plane,
And both differ from the commuters.
As passengers settle on seats,
A distinct seat the driver takes too,
As the duty is specific.
With no direct burden on the body,
This duty he does on terms understood by all parties.
And from take-off to destination,
Passengers' characteristics must be constant,
The weight and identity remain same.
And when the journey is rather long,
The stretch is broken to unwind and refuel.
Mother is the most wonderful pilot.
She is the vehicle that carries the passenger within herself.
Her passenger listens to no terms,
And therefore metamorphoses without notices.
What about glands and hormones and their dynamism?
The glands seek no permission to produce,
The hormones transport without apologies,
All within the poor vessel called Mother.

Unlike a climber approaching the peak of a mountain and having a clearer view,
Of the surrounding and the peak ahead,
Mother is the climber who gradually becomes the mountain with no spectacle opportunity
To know what's happening within self.
Endurance, perseverance, long-suffering, patience, faith and love constitute the strength
Of this amazing pilot who God uses as channel to bring us down here.
What a wonderful pilot mother is!

8-facts-you-need-to-know-about-virgin-mary

Mother Mary (Maryam)

The mother of Jesus Christ of Nazareth who went about doing good. The embarrassment caused by the circumstances surrounding her conception of Jesus notwithstanding, Blessed Virgin Mary found the courage to have Baby Jesus. She had to flee from her base when the king found the star of the baby threatening and determined to kill Jesus.

She was aware of her son's gift and she encouraged him to use them; for instance she brought it to His notice that wine had finished at the wedding in Cana of Galilee. She was there standing by him till the end when he was being crucified.

14

Northern Star

If anyone sees Sister Perpetual,
Tell her she bears Mother's name.
Perpetual is mother's love;
Ever stable and unbroken.
Your mother's known name may be Jibowu, Elizabeth or Aisha,
Seek to know her more,
And you will find Lady Constance!
A mother's love is ever constant,
Like the northern star.
Such is the love of Monica for Augustine, her son.
Oh Mother Monica, wife of Patricius, mother of Augustine, the saint,
She prayed and wept over her son's sins,
Augustine who had taken to a wild life,
"It is not possible that the son of many tears should perish,"
So says a sympathetic Bishop.
An unfriendly mother-in-law, an inconsistent husband,
And a wayward son with strange views;
All, Monica coped with!
So sick as a child was Augustine,

That Monica was distressed,
Her joy and relief at Augustine's recovery turned to anxiety,
As he misspent his renewed life being wayward and lazy.
The disciplinarian part of Monica says;
"Go from my table!"
That is a strong woman speaking.
Convicted by a dream she had,
Monica reached out again,
That is a tenderly mother listening,
To her own prophetic instincts.
And Monica followed her wayward son to Rome,
Where he had gone secretly,
But he had gone to Millan,
Yet Monica followed him.
Monica endured seventeen years of resistance
And it paid off,
The joy of seeing Augustine convert to the good that she knew
Brought the ultimate joy.
Mother and son spent six months of true peace,
And death overtook Monica, all of her physical strength spent!
All on her family!
Oh sweet Mother's love; sweet is your continual flow.
Stable, non-stop and immutable is Mother's precious love!

saintmonica

Mother Monica

Mother Monica coped with a difficult mother-in-law, a drunkard husband and a wayward son with strange views. Her Mothering task was huge but she faced it squarely. Augustine, her son, who made her cry many times, changed for the better and he is today known and referred to as Saint Augustine.

The Child of many tears did not perish. Monica herself was canonized and is today looked up to as patron saint of mothers who find child-raising tasking and in need of strength to cope.

15

Prophet

Had Monica belonged to the group that says,
I dream not,
Child of many tears would have perished!
What mother seeks repose while the task is yet
unaccomplished?
Though never listed,
To watch and to pray is prime among mother's duties.
As a bride, the Holy Spirit is the groom that Mother
expects always;
Morning, afternoon, evening and night,
Midnight, midday, dusk and dawn.
Mothering is spiritual!
Mothering is prophetic!
She watches, she prays,
She thinks, she introspects,
She reflects, she anticipates,
She meditates, she contemplates,
She foresees, she foretells,
She accords, she rewards, she blesses!
She invokes and confers divine favour on her seed.
And her spirit sings!
Her songs pull down, her songs destroy.
Her songs plant, her songs build.

Her songs raise, her songs elevate.
Her songs permeate, her songs pierce.
Her songs fly, her songs travel.
Where mother sings, principalities flee.
Mother never goes on leave,
Her mothering ministry operates on all lands in all weathers.
She admonishes, she encourages.
Yet she takes no break,
And she is very true.
Oh darling, sweet, precious, blessed mother,
How kind thou art,
A worthy prophet.

Adunni Atoori-bi-Opo

Adunni Atoori-bi-Opo

Her mothering burden was huge and she did so much alone. Her labour of love on her children was incomparable, yet she had the capacity to extend love to all; friends and foes alike to the point that a high chief from her hometown who she had mentored, said at her funeral, "If one begins to tell stories of the life and times of aunty, it will be dusk and dawn many times over; aunty is one of those that some people refer to as Malaika but many would never be conscious of it until they are gone!"

Her live-and-let-others-live spirit is the greatest inheritance that her children got from her. She was a giver to a fault. She left a legacy of love for all, devotion to God and courage to live.

16

Worthy of Care

She carried the child in her womb for months caring
for the foetus.
She sacrificed her favourites;
Food, wears, scents, and practices,
Yet she cares!
She became a stranger to herself that the child may
be well,
She walked through the valley of the shadow of death
in labour,
Yet she cares!
She suffered post-partum symptoms and pains,
Yet she cares!
She cared for the child day and night at the expense of
her own care and sleep.
She rationalised her resources while she starved that
the child may lack nothing.
She stayed awake tired because the child was awake
and must be watched,
Truly she cares!
Her laps, her back, her chest are available to the child
as cushion regardless of her feelings and her state of
health.
Yes, she cares!

Her breast is the child's first food source and many times she is sucked famished.

Her nipples are the child's first chewing practice tool.

Her teeth are the child's first meat grinder.

She abandoned her own meals to force-feed and spoon-feed the child when the child couldn't feed self.

Her clothes and body received the child's faeces and urine to her pleasure,

Ooh, she cares!

Other people around moved away detesting the smell of the child's releases but mother stays to face it happen.

She cleaned the child throughout the period when the child couldn't clean self.

She dresses up the child to the best of her resources and ability that the child may be presentable and found appealing by all.

She lullabies the child to sleep while she works on to get the child's need ready before wake.

She saves, depriving herself so much to buy her child the nicest things among the child's peers.

She stays alert in her spirit non-stop to plead God to action on every issue surrounding the child.

She watches when and where the child's peers are ripe for school, work, marriage, recognition, elevation, acquisition, and procreation.

She nudges hers to action promptly on all relevant issues that hers may be ahead of the pack.

She cares still about everything relating to her child even when the child becomes independent.
The care burden of her grandchildren she co-shoulders that her child may be at ease.
Mother cares in the morning,
She cares still by the midday,
She cares in the afternoon,
Mother cares still at dusk,
She cares through the evening,
Mother cares still in the midnight,
...And she cares through to the dawn.
Be it ante meridiem or post meridiem, mother cares!
Mother is the most worthy of care.
The one who cares for each and all,
Deserves care by all.
Yes, each and every one and everybody.
Mother cares truly and deeply.
... And truly she deserves care from the farthest depth of grateful hearts.
Mother is worthy of care.
Should I be made rich in this world, I shall take care of my mother.

Madam Asabi Adedire

Asabi Adedire

Madam Asabi Adedire was a Nigerian mother from Ile-Ife who volunteered to donate her kidney to her ailing son in faraway Michigan without an understanding of what kidney transplant was.

She only asked whether her son, Abraham Adedire, would live thereafter without any question on what would become of the donor. Her son got well after a successful surgery and resumed work in Michigan as mother returned to Ile-Ife Nigeria only to learn later that her son was dead. He fell ill a while after and died, with reports that his kidneys were functioning well as at the time of his death. Who can ever know Asabi's pain?

17
Pleasurable to Have

It is sweet having a mother.
Having a mother is pleasurable.
To have a mother is enjoyable.
Delightful is it to have a mother.
Nothing is more relaxing than having a mother.
It's so comfortable having a mother.
That one has a mother pays.
There is bliss in having a mother.
Being with Mother is peaceful.
Looking up to Mother is interesting.
Being guarded by Mother is a blessing.
To be guided by Mother is an opportunity.
Being nurtured by Mother is grace.
Mother is the unparalleled asset to have.
Mother's love is inestimable.
It is frabjous having a mother.
Mother's love is sweet, delightful, enjoyable, marvelous, satisfying, fantastic and fabulous!
Mother, the one with a glorious heart!

Abisola Olayemi Williams

Abisola Olayemi Williams

Mummy Williams is an amazing mother with astounding capacity to love and give. Her husband from her youth with whom she had and raised four successful children suffered a prolonged illness for the last years of his life, while Mummy Williams took charge of the burden for two in addition to the trauma of her closest friend's ailment.

As a retired frontline female permanent secretary from the federal civil service of Nigeria, her administrative acumen and natural brilliance paid off in managing the family estate and preserving essential relationships and networks while her husband received care. Her devotion to her husband left none of the children, all of whom are raising their respective families, with no other option than to keep loving and caring for their father till the end.

Her first child and first daughter has publicly and with pride described her as the proverbs-31 woman at many events. Her children take after her compassion and two of them, a social worker and a medical doctor run successful charity organisations in their respective locations of Nigeria and United States of America. Mummy Williams is gracious within and benevolent without. The marriage between one of her sons and her friend's daughter points to the fact that the seed of a woman noted for good deeds can be trusted.

This blessed mother honours motherhood in multiple ways. She blesses the memory of her pilot to the world with the naming of her credible firm, Selina Ventures after her own mother. This super motherly octogenarian lives a decent retirement life in Lagos, Nigeria. Mummy Williams has an impressive number of adopted children and mentees in addition to her biological children. One of her grandchildren once wrote about her: "My grandmother is a very kind and generous woman with a beautiful smile. Any time I think of her, her smiling face appears and I begin to smile too."

18

Retires Not

She started singing as a young girl to her unborn child.
She was quick to raise her hand in prayer,
Everywhere the challenge was thrown;
To know who desired to be mother one day.
Even when the daunting tasks were listed,
She enlisted!
She knew of breastfeeding, home training and school training,
And she was not discouraged.
She saw the end from pre-beginning times,
As she sang of how her fruits yet unborn would inherit her possessions.
She bathed and fed doll babies as rehearsals of actual mothering.
She created attraction and won the necessary attention.
She was there and submissive to accept the imported ingredient,
That would complete the local recipe of her reproductive factory.
She accommodated the ingredient supplier and hosted the formation for nine good months,

60 seconds every minute,
60 minutes every hour,
24 hours every day,
7 days every week,
4 weeks every month,
30 days every month,
90 days every trimester.
270 days of gestation she was on duty throughout without exception of any moment.
She was on duty pre-labour and in labour.
She was on duty pre-natal and post natal.
She serves the infant, the toddler and the child,
She serves the pre-teen, the teenager, the adolescent and the youth,
She serves the learner, the worker-in-training and the officer,
Yet she serves her child as single, unmarried, about to marry and as married,
She serves her child as awaiting parent and as parent,
She serves as grandma still to her child's child.
Service continues through the entirety of her lifetime.
And in death, her soul works on.
She blesses her children here on earth as an individual defender,
In death, she joins the league of translated mothers
Who support one another.
In favour of her descendants left behind here on earth,

Mother watches on!
Mother works from conception to death; she never retires!

Love Works

Fruits

An expectant mother is advised to eat fruits, and a lactating mother finds fruits handy when hunger strikes amidst her tight schedule. Mother does so much with fruits; she eats fruits and gives fruits to the Fruits of her womb. Mother knows the fruit type that each child loves, the reason she buys a variety at a time. Mother, the fruitful giver of fruits in every way.

19

Knower

The sole knows the earth.
The door sees within and without.
The skull and the hair are no strangers to each other.
The sand knows the ocean.
The sky knows vapour.
The blind knows darkness.
The lion knows its cub.
Mother knows the child from conception through gestation to delivery and beyond.
Mother feeds the child by the fluid of her own body from within her own womb.
Mother knows the child before the arrival of the child on its first day.
The womb felt the kick,
From nipple grips to suckle-time excitement and suckle-time attitude.
Mother knows the child before the child's censor starts self-image management.
A mother knows her child more than the child knows self.
Your Mother knows YOU!

Yam tuber

When her wallet permits her to pick either thirst-quenching ice-cream during working hours or a stomach-filling tuber of yam, that her child may have dinner, Mother would rather go for the tuber.

20

Pillar

From the formless and spineless state at inception,
When the zygote had got no bones,
Mother is the pillar.
Oh yes, the pillar on which the formation rests to develop.
Oh yes, the pillar that bears the child's burden like no other.
At the feeble stage as an infant,
Her palms, her chest, her back serve the child as bed to lay.
From crèche to pre-school, from high school to college,
From matriculation to graduation,
From degree to designation, mother is!
From bearable weight of a toddler to adult size of overwhelming weight,
Her support remains constant.
In diverse forms, mother's support comes;
Physical, social and psychological.
A deep-rooted spiritual pillar she is too.
A tall pillar with real height transcending the physical appearance mother is.
So deep, so firm, so stable, so strong,

So trustworthy, so reliable, so dependable,
Irremovable, irreplaceable and enduring.
What a marvelous pillar mother is!

Working class women in the market

Working-class Mother rushes down to the market at break time. Closing time and off-days too are spent sourcing for the needs of her family. She does all in love and with love.

21
Considerate

Mother eats after her child has eaten.
Mother won't sleep if her child doesn't sleep.
She would rather go searching in the dark than have her child trapped outside;
She would rather dare the looming dangers.
She would rather buy the child's school wears than renew her wardrobe.
She would rather remain the guard at the door,
Than go to answer the call of nature;
Lest the threat advances to the child's hiding place.
She would rather have her child take away the umbrella,
Than keep it for herself against the next rains.
She would rather live serving and starving,
Than go after the greener pasture leaving her child unattended.
She considers the comfort of her child first.
All hail Mother!

Market shot

Sometimes she is selling, sometimes she is buying, yet Mother plans, serves and gives.

22

Benevolent Predecessor

Mother is a benevolent predecessor.
She does not live her descendants with complicated relationships,
In her lifetime and in death,
The child benefits from all that is Mother's.
In death, Mother's soul blesses and blesses and blesses on.
Her possessions are meant for and inherited by products of one womb.
Her children are her children.
She has got only one womb which announces everything it carries.
Pregnancy and birth automatically align the fruits of her womb for her inheritance.
The pregnancy is her pronouncement that the child that shall be born shall be entitled to her estate as her child.
No law deprives a child from inheriting Mother's asset regardless of the status of marriage or circumstances of birth.
Her womb is the law which accommodates every child born of it.

She does not and cannot hide or deny what emanated from her womb.
Mother is a benevolent ancestor.

Mud-pot/mortar-pestle

Mother transfers everything she has got down the line, her assets, her skills, her creativity, her clientele and her goodwill.

23
Heritage

A child's maternity is the ever genuine inheritance.
A legacy, a right, a status that can never be disputed.
A heritage that can never be withdrawn, suspended or denied.
Neither can it ever be terminated, by any means; psychic, social or legal.
How wise the matrilineal societies are!
Paternal identity can change,
Every connection deriving from the changed identity too.
Maternity and every connection that derive from it are forever!
When the paternal relations dislike a child's mother,
The child is stigmatized too,
Whereas when a child's maternal relations consider the child's father unworthy,
They draw the child closer!
They keep hope in the child and support the child through life.
With your father, you win by your mother.
With your mother, you win all ways.
Mother is a dependable and eternal heritage.

Booli vendor

The environment notwithstanding, Mother labours on towards the actualization of her beautiful dreams; she ekes out a living no matter what.

24

Undeniable

One's mother is one's mother,
Let her be.
Who is that child admiring the pretty next-door
woman?
Oh, you have seen another kinder than your mother?
And she appears to you as humane and hospitable?
And you rely on her connections and brilliance?
Let her wealth and generosity grow without bounds,
Let her turn more religious or beneficial than she is
today,
She remains "that woman";
A title for the woman far off but never for Mother.
There will always be "this" and "that" woman here
and there, now and then.
Mother is Mother!
Never tag her labour cloths unpresentable.
The heavens assign Mother and the earth leaves it so.
One's mother is one's mother.
She who is not one's mother will never be one's
mother.
By divorce marriage is dissolved,
Friends can be changed with time and at will,
Paternity can change with a mother's confession,

And the DNA test to prove,
But nothing changes Mother, Never!
Neither denial nor legal proceedings,
Psychic wisdom nor anything anywhere anytime anyhow,
Is capable of changing who one's mother is.
Mother is indeed undeniable.

Fish vendor

Come rain, come sunshine, unrestingly, Mother labours day and night; faith, hope and love are the secret of her strength.

25

May I Be Blessed

I shall receive blessings by my mother's mouth.
No, no, never a curse!
Always will I be blessed by my Mother's soul.
In my favour shall it function,
Mama's motherhood unction day and night.
May I be blessed by the soul of she who knew me
before I knew self.
Bless me, O Mama, and I am blessed.
I shall be blessed by the mouth of her whose love I
can trust.
I shall be blessed by the mouth of her from whose
womb I emerged.
I shall be blessed by the mouth of her who gazed
upon my heavy eye in sickness.
I shall be blessed by the mouth of her who carried me
when no one else could.
I shall be blessed by the mouth of her who wishes me
well the most.
I shall be blessed every moment every time by
Mother.
I shall be blessed by her who cares for me as Mother
and as Angel.

I shall be blessed by her who feels enormous joy that I am well.

I shall be blessed by her who can never forsake me.

Bless me Mother that I may find favour with Man and with God.

I will be good, Mother, and make you happy.

The days of childishness shall be over.

Your love shall see me through,

As God's love leads me on.

So help me God.

So, help me Holy Spirit Divine,

Help the child's foolishness and aid Mama's maturity.

Ingredients

No one can serve as much soup on the child's meal as Mother does. Mother makes most delicious soups from a combination of ordinary ingredients, each of which gives no clue on its own until Mother's mastery comes to play. How resourceful Mother is! The master passes this culinary skill and discipline to future mothers too.

26

Teacher

A heaven-ordained teacher she is.
Without mother's initial lessons to the child,
School teachers will find it tougher.
Mother is the teacher before the teachers.
She laid you down to sleep, teaching you to lay right.
She lullabies you, teaching you to sing.
She pats you to sleep, teaching you to care.
She carried you from sleep, teaching you to rise.
She bathes you, teaching you to clean.
She dresses you, teaching you to cover.
She talks to you, teaching you to speak.
She feeds you, teaching you to eat.
She chews your meat bites, teaching you to masticate.
She introduces others to you, teaching you courtesy.
She makes you touch your body parts, telling you
what each is called,
That you may know yourself.
She makes you identify the parts again and again,
That you may not forget.
She leads you to engage your hands for specific
purposes,
That you may distinguish between the two hands.

She teaches you to sit right, talk right, walk right, act right,
That you may be respectable.
She teaches you ethics, labour, preservation and sowing and reaping,
That you may have a meaningful life.
She leads you in the path of self-actualization and independence.
She introduced your dad to you.
She teaches you to socialize, that you may not be odd.
She gives you your first language of expression called mother-tongue.
She teaches, guides and leads.
O precious Mother,
Incomparable counsellor and torch bearer,
Blessed art thou forever more!

Image References

Albert, S. (How to Grow Apples, N.d.). *Apple_tree_with_fruit-1* [Photograph]. Harvest to Table. https://harvesttotable.com/how_to_grow_apples_/ Accessed on 10th Aug., 2020.

Babangida M. (Message from the Founder Dr (Mrs) Maryam Babangida, N.d.). *Founder* [Photograph]. El-Amin International School. http://www.el-aminschool.com/the-founder.php Accessed on 11th Aug., 2020.

Bissanti G. (Agaricus bisporus, 11th Sept. 2018). *Agaricus_bisporus-800x445* [Photograph]. Un Mondo Ecosostenibile (An Ecosustainable World). https://antropocene.it/en/2018/09/11/agaricus-bisporus/ Accessed on 11th Aug., 2020.

Cocoparisienne. (N.d.). *dove-2516641_1280* [Photograph]. Pixabay. www.pixabay.com/photos/dove-bird-animal-feather-plumage-2516641/ Accessed on 11th Aug., 2020.

Mishkov A. (8 Facts You Need to Know about Virgin Mary, 2016). *8-facts-you-need-to-know-about-virgin-mary* [Computer graphics]. DocumentaryTube.
https://www.documentarytube.com/articles/8-facts-you-need-to-know-about-virgin-mary Accessed on 11th Aug., 2020.

Oladele I. (2020). *Akoko tree* [Photograph]. Ado-Ekiti, Nigeria. JPEG.

Oladele I. (2020). *Coconut tree* [Photograph]. Ado-Ekiti, Nigeria. JPEG.

Oladele I. (2020). *Igi Arere* [Photograph]. Ado-Ekiti, Nigeria. JPEG.

Oladele I. (2020). *Kola nut tree* [Photograph]. Ado-Ekiti, Nigeria. JPEG.

Oladele I. (2020). *Odan tree* [Photograph]. Ado-Ekiti, Nigeria. JPEG.

Oladele I. (2020). *Osun tree* [Photograph]. Ado-Ekiti, Nigeria. JPEG.

Oladele I. (2020). *Palm tree* [Photograph]. Ado-Ekiti, Nigeria. JPEG.

Omotayo A. (2001). *Adunni Atoori-bi-Opo* [Photograph]. Ado-Ekiti, Nigeria. JPEG.

Omotayo A. (2020). *Booli vendor* [Photograph]. Garki International Market, Abuja, Nigeria. JPEG.

Omotayo A. (2020). *Fish vendor* [Photograph]. Garki International Market, Abuja, Nigeria. JPEG.

Omotayo A. (2020). *Fruits* [Photograph]. Abuja, Nigeria. JPEG.

Omotayo A. (2020). *Ingredients* [Photograph]. Garki, Abuja, Nigeria. JPEG.

Omotayo A. (2020). *Market shot* [Photograph]. Garki International Market, Abuja, Nigeria. JPEG.

Omotayo A. (2020). *Mud-pot/mortar-pestle* [Photograph]. Garki International Market, Abuja, Nigeria. JPEG.

Omotayo A. (2020). *Neem tree* [Photograph]. Abuja, Nigeria. JPEG.

Omotayo A. (2020). *Working class women in the market* [Photograph]. Garki International Market, Abuja, Nigeria. JPEG.

Omotayo A. (2020). *Yam tuber* [Photograph]. Abuja, Nigeria. JPEG.

Onigegewura O. (Ife Boy in Michigan: The Extraordinary Story of a Mother's Love by

Onigegewura, 10th July, 2018). *Madam Asabi Adedire* [Photograph]. Onigegewura. http://onigegewura.blogspot.com/2018/07/ife-boy-in-michigan-extraordinary-story.html?m=1 Accessed on 11th Aug., 2020.

Spadefoot Nursery. (Arizona Is Bananas? 2019). *banana+flower* [Photograph]. Spadefoot Nursery. https://www.spadefootnursery.com/blog/2019/12/30/arizona-is-bananas Accessed on 11th Aug., 2020.

Spadefoot Nursery. (Arizona Is Bananas? 2019). *image-asset* [Photograph]. Spadefoot Nursery. https://www.spadefootnursery.com/blog/2019/12/30/arizona-is-bananas Accessed on 11th Aug., 2020.

St. Monica Parish. (Who Is Saint Monica? N.d.). *saintmonica* [Painting]. St. Monica Parish. https://www.st-monica.org/patron-saint Accessed on 11th Aug., 2020.

Williams O. (2017). *Abisola Olayemi Williams* [Photograph]. Lagos, Nigeria. JPEG.

The Author

Adebola Abeni Omotayo is a Nigerian writer.

She joined The Broadcasting Service of Ekiti State as a duty continuity announcer and later served in almost all the units of both the Programmes Department and the News and Current Affairs Department. The bi-lingual presenter anchored many shows in both English and Yoruba languages on both the radio and television arms of the same establishment to the pleasure of the corporation's teeming audience.

She was Chairman, Nigeria Association of Women Journalists (NAWOJ), Ekiti State Chapter, between 2004 and 2008. She had a stint with The British Department for International Development (DFID) as a Project Support Person while the Department was assisting The Ekiti State Government to produce its first Poverty Reduction Strategy Paper, The State Economic Empowerment and Development Strategy (SEEDS) document.

In 2005, she founded Heritage for Posterity HEPO, an NGO which started out with interest in children and youth but later expanded its scope to cover the preservation of every beneficial thing that symbolises heritage.

Bola Omotayo delights in teaching and her areas of interest include entrepreneurship, culture and moral values as well as parenting.

She is a member of The Ekiti State Tree Growers Association, EKSTGA.

Bola Omotayo is a wife and a mother and she lives a quiet life with her family in Abuja, Nigeria.

She is also the author of **'Beyond the Box'** and **'Negligence No More'**.

The Book

Love Song to Mother is a compilation of the author's original compositions depicting everybody's mother.

In this book, there is a picture of every mother in the world, yet it is clearer than what any conventional photographer can capture as the deepest traits and attributes of Mother are all covered.

As a child, neither have you offered the best gift to your mother nor kept a memoir in her honour until you come across the book Love Song to Mother. It is also a soothing balm that any mother can keep nearby at all times either she has received the copy as a gift or she has procured it by herself.